Bridging the Gap between us and our children

Donovan Davis
5036 Dr. Phillips Blvd. Suite 124
Orlando, Florida 32819

Bridging the gap between us and our children
First Edition
2025 by Donovan Davis

ISBN: 978-09802391-1-9

<u>Acknowledgments</u>

First I would like to thank my lord and savior Jesus Christ for inspiring me to write this book. Second, I'll be honest, it is hard for me to write acknowledgments for the simple reason that my life as an father has been blessed with a multitude of parental influences. Of course, I have to begin with the love of my life Marquita. It's been a wonderful experience having you in my life, your calming spirit makes me a better person. I can't imagine spending the rest of my life with anyone else.

To my children Desire and Destiny, you girls are growing up so fast, and I love you both dearly. To my mother I miss you dearly and I wish you could be here to enjoy this accomplishment. I love you always and I know you are watching over me.

Special thanks to my fraternity brothers the men of Phi Beta Sigma Fraternity, Inc. and Zeta Phi Beta Sorority, Inc.

To some of my mother's closest friends Lillie Thomas, Mildred Singleton, and Mary McCloud who are all excellent parents, thank you for being a positive and influential guide of what true parenting is all about.

If I didn't mention someone please don't take it personal, blame it on the head, and not the heart.

Thank you to Vincent Palmer for an awesome web site www.askdonovandavis.com

Table of Contents

Today's Situation 7

Relationships 8

Different Kinds of Relationships 12

Discipline 24

Developing Self Control 27

How to discipline effectively 32

Drug Talk 36

Discussing Divorce 42

Gangs 77

Self- Esteem Section 82

Resolving Conflict Section 89

Decision Making Section 93

Social Media Section 100

Bullying Section 110

Sexting   117

Goal Setting Section   120

Self Esteem Activities for the Home135

Synopsis   149

<u>**Today's Situation**</u>

1. Parents or adults have you lost touch with our kids?
2. Parents or adults do you need to improve your relationship with our children?
3. Parents or adults would you like for your kids to talk to you when they have a problem?
If you answered yes to any of these questions you have invested in the right training session.

How Did We Get Here?
We all are working hard everyday and sometimes our kids receive the least amount of attention. Our children need us and we are going to look at four key elements of importance:
1. Daily Schedule
2. Relationships
3. Mirror Effect
4. Maximum Effort

Daily Family Schedule
<u>**Monday - Friday**</u>
Work 9:00 to 5:00
Children Pick-Up 5:00 to 6:30
Dinner preparation 6:30 to 7:00
Family Dinner 7:00 to 7:30
Kids Bath 7:30 to 8:00
Parents time w/ kids 8:00 to 8:30
Kids Bed time 8:30

<u>**REALITY**</u>

The previous schedule shows only an hour and thirty minutes of direct quality time for kids each day.

<u>**Relationships**</u>

Relationships are essential to the progress of human growth.

<u>**Parent / Teacher**</u>

A positive parent/ teacher relationship will improve our children behavior within the classroom.

<u>**Parent / Child**</u>

A positive parent / child relationship will increase your connection with our children at home and at school.

OTHER RELATIONSHIPS

Husband / Wife

A happy marriage will display to our children that marriage does work, and your marriage will be there point of reference on how to make a marriage work.

Teacher / Child

A successful teacher/ child relationship will insure that our children are learning in the educational environment.

All of the above are relationships that are vital to our positive progress in life.

Mirror Effect

The mirror effect essentially is "treat people the way you want to be treated".

If you didn't like for your parents or teachers to disrespect you then you definitely shouldn't disrespect our children.

Look into your life mirror and remember that you weren't a perfect child, but what worked on you then will work now.

If you look into your life mirror, make sure you recall the things that you didn't grow from and don't repeat them.

Maximum Effort

Each day we are faced with an opportunity to spend quality time with our future which is our children.

The effort we display to children is crucial to the success of our relationship.

The relationship may not be important to you, but the relationship may mean everything to that child.

In each place I have worked, love has overruled all

negative situations. The effort you put in to loving

our children should be maximum effort.

What elements of our character should we display to children?

 The five elements are:
1. Unconditional Love
2. Unconditional Patience
3. Guidance or consulting
4. Coaching
5. Supervision

Different Kinds of Relationships

There are different kinds of attachment relationships that can be put into different categories. These categories can describe children's relationships with both parents and childcare providers. Research has found that there are at least four attachment categories. The categories describe the ways that children act and the ways that adults act with the children. The strongest kind of attachment is called 'secure.' The way a parent or provider responds a child may lead to one of the four types of attachment categories. The way a child is attached to her parents also affects how she will behave around others when her parent is not around.

1. Disorganized relationships. Disorganized children don't know what to expect from their parents. Children with relationships in the other categories have organized attachments. This means that they have all learned ways to get what they need, even if it is not the best way. This happens because a child learns to predict how his parent will react, whether it is positive or negative. They also learn that doing certain things will make their parents do certain things.

• Disorganized children will do things that seem to make no sense.

• Sometimes these children will speak really fast and will be hard to understand.

• Most disorganized children have a hard time understanding the feelings of other children.

• Disorganized children who are playing with dolls might act out scenes that are confusing and scary.

• Disorganized children may be very hard to understand. They may seem very different from day to day.

What kind of parent behavior is linked to this category of attachment?

• The parents rarely respond to their needs when they are infants.

• If the parent does respond, the response usually does not fit.

• It is common for disorganized children to come

from families in which some form of neglect or maltreatment is happening.

• It is also possible that these children may have one or more parents suffering from depression.

2. Ambivalent relationships. Ambivalence (not being completely sure of something) is another way a child may be insecurely attached to his parents. Children who are ambivalent have learned that sometimes their needs are met, and sometimes they are not. They notice what behavior got their parents' attention in the past and use it over and over. They are always looking for that feeling of security that they sometimes get.

• Ambivalent children are often very clingy.

• They tend to act younger than they really are and may seem over-emotional.

• When older preschoolers or early-elementary children want an adult's attention, they might use baby talk or act like a baby.

• Ambivalent children often cry, get frustrated easily, and love to be the center of attention.

• They get upset if people aren't paying attention to them and have a hard time doing things on their own.

• Ambivalent children seem to latch onto everyone for short periods of time.

• They have a very hard time letting parents go at

the beginning of the day, and the crying may last a long time.

What kind of parent behavior is linked to this category of attachment?

• When an infant is crying, these parents sometimes respond; sometimes they don't.

• When a child is hungry, she might be fed, but it is more likely that she will be fed when she's not hungry.

• When a child is frightened, she is ignored sometimes and overly comforted at other times.

• When a child is excited about something, a parent doesn't understand the child's excitement or responds to her in a way that does not fit.

3. Avoidant relationships. This is one category of attachment that is not secure. Avoidant children have learned that depending on parents won't get them that secure feeling they want, so they learn to take care of themselves.

• Avoidant children may seem too independent.

 • They do not often ask for help, but they get frustrated easily.

• They may have difficulty playing with other children their age. They may be aggressive at times.

• Biting, hitting, pushing, and screaming are common for many children, but avoidant children do those things more than other children.

• Avoidant children usually do not build strong relationships with providers in their childcare setting.

• They don't complain when the parents leave them, and they usually do not greet them when the parents return. They know that the parents have returned, but it is almost like they want to punish them by ignoring them.

• They seem to try to care for themselves.

What kind of parent behavior is linked to this category of attachment?

• Parents respond to their children's needs, but it usually takes a while.

• When a child is hungry, the child will be fed, but probably after she's been waiting for a long time.

• When a child is frightened, she is usually left to deal with it on her own.

• When a child is excited about something, the parent may turn away or ignore her.

• The child gets used to not having her needs met, so she learns to take care of herself.

There are different reasons why parents might act this way. Some parents just don't know when their baby or child needs something. Other parents might think that it will make their child more independent if the parents do not give in to the child.

4. Secure relationships. This is the strongest type of attachment. A child in this category feels he can depend on his parent. He knows that person will be there when he needs support. He knows what to expect.

• The secure child usually plays well with other children his age.

• He may cry when his mother leaves. He will usually settle down if a friendly adult is there to comfort him.

• When parents pick him up from childcare, he is usually very happy to see them.

 • He may have a hard time leaving childcare, though. This can be confusing if the child was upset when the parents left at the beginning of the day. It does not mean that the child is not happy to see the parents.

How do adults build secure attachment relationships?

• Adults are consistent when they respond to the child's needs.

• When a child cries, the adult responds in a lovingly or caring way.

• When a child is hungry, the adult feeds her fairly soon.

• When a child is afraid, the adult is there to take care of her.

• When the child is excited about something, the adults are excited about it, too.

Over time, a securely attached child has learned that he can rely on special adults to be there for him. He knows that, if he ever needs something, someone will be there to help. A child who believes this can then learn other things. He will use special adults as a secure base. He will smile at the adult and come to her to get a hug. Then he will move out and explore his world.

Note about different cultures: Parents and other caregivers show love in different ways in different cultures. In any culture, though, children can have good relationships with parents and providers. In all cultures, adults can build secure attachments if they are sensitive and respond to children's signals. The way they respond will be very different from one culture to another, however. Providers who work with children from different cultures should watch for differences. Ask parents and other people from that culture how they care for children.

Discipline

What is discipline and the goals of discipline?
•Discipline means teaching and training.

The Goals of Good Discipline:
•To encourage appropriate behavior.
•To help prevent problems from arising as the child grows older.
•To instill a lifelong sense of self-discipline.

Why is discipline important?
•Discipline is the key to the way your child will behave.

Why should I focus on discipline today?
•Appropriate and consistent discipline can make life smoother and more pleasant for you, your child and everyone in the family.

How will the discipline I teach my child today affect their behavior tomorrow?
•The way discipline is handled in your family will help shape the kind of adult your child will become in the future.

Discipline is an on going process!!
•It begins early in the child's life.
•It involves changes as the child matures.
•It continues until the child is an adult, and then goes on as self-discipline.

How does discipline help in the development of our children?

Discipline helps children:
1. Develop self-control
2. Express emotions appropriately
3. Respect others' rights
4. Build self-esteem
5. Become self-reliant
6. Develop orderliness

Developing Self-Control

•Feelings of anger, jealousy, helplessness and fear are only natural at times. They may surface as temper tantrums, whining or fighting.

•Parents can help their children handle these feelings constructively.

Express Emotions Appropriately

•It's not always easy to say "I'm sorry" or "That hurt my feelings." Talking about feelings can help prevent misunderstanding and bitterness.

Respect Others' Rights

•Everyone has the right to privacy, to be spoken to politely and to have personal belongings left alone. Children should be taught to say "please" and "thank you", to knock before entering a room, and to respect others belongings.

Build Self-Esteem

•Children need attention and praise when they behave well. This helps reinforce good feelings about themselves.

Become Self-Reliant

•Children need to learn how to take care of themselves (dress, wash, etc.) and to do simple household tasks. Mastering these skills helps children develop confidence in their abilities.

Develop Orderliness

•Good work habits help children succeed at home, at school and, as an adult, at work. Don't excuse repeat forgetfulness, messiness as part of a child's

personality.

Why do children misbehave?

<u>At times they misbehave because:</u>
•They were never clearly told that a certain behavior
was wrong.

There are four areas that may be the cause of
misbehavior:
➢ Anger
➢ Hurt
➢Fear
➢Jealousy

<u>Anger</u>

•Children may become angry when they don't get

what they want. If parents give in to angry demands,

the child learns the anger "works" and will continue

to use it.

Hurt

•Feelings of hurt or disappointment can linger for a long time. Children may seek revenge against people they feel let them down.

Fear

•Children may be afraid of many things (darkness, new people, failing in school, losing their parents' love, etc.) Sometimes their actions are misinterpreted as deliberate misbehavior.

Jealousy

•Children may be jealous of a new baby or brother's or sister's accomplishment. They may use misbehavior to get attention.

Negative Parenting patterns

•Your child makes a demand: "I want some candy."

•You as a parent refuses to give your child candy, pointing out that it's almost dinner time.

•Your child's demands continue: "But I still want candy!"

•You the parent becomes irritated.

•Your child keeps pestering for the candy.

•We as the parent gets upset and overreacts.

•We as parents feel guilty, apologizes to the child, and gives the candy after all.

We must break this cycle!!!!!!!

<u># How to discipline effectively</u>

Encourage positive behavior through these basic steps:

➢ *Give children love*

➢*Listen to your children*

➢*Understand your child*

➢*Set limits*

➢*Give rewards*

➢*Promote Independence*

➢*Discuss emotions*

➢*Promote Responsibility*

<u>Give children love</u>

•All children need to know they are loved. Younger children especially need the reassurance of hugs, kisses, smiles and praise. Immediate praise encourages children to repeat positive behavior.

Listen to your children

•Adults like attention when they speak, and so do children! Listen carefully to your child. Your child may be flattered by your interest and try even harder to please you.

•Busy parents should set aside a special listening time each day. For example, talk together during a walk, while doing the dishes or before bedtime.

Understand your child

•Needs and wants change as children grow older. For example, young children need to know parents are near. Most teenagers need some privacy as well as regular outings with friends. Listening and observing carefully will help prepare you to deal with these changes.

Set Limits

•Realistic limits are necessary for safety and for the family's happiness.

Setting limits involves:

➢Explanation

➢Discussion

➢Repetition

Explanation

•Share with children the reasons for proposed limits.

Discussion

•Coming to an agreement on the need for the limits, and ensuring that the limits are understood.

<u>**Repetition**</u>

•Reminding children about limits until self-discipline develops. Children may test you to see if you're serious. At other times, they may simply forget what they're supposed to do.

The whole family needs limits on:

•Time (bedtime, curfews)

•Boundaries (you may go here but not there)

•Behavior (you may do this, but not that)

•Enforce limits firmly and fairly!!!!!!!!

Drug Talk

<u>Drug Talk</u>

What do you say?

➢Tell them that you love them and you want them to be healthy and happy.

➢Say you do not find alcohol and other illegal drug use acceptable. Many parents never state this simple principle.

➢Explain how this use hurts people.

➢Discuss the legal issues.

➢Talk about positive drug free alternatives.

How do you say it?

❖Calmly and openly- don't exaggerate.

The facts speak for themselves.

❖Face to face- exchange information and try to understand each other's point of view. Be an active listener and let your child talk about fears and concerns. Don't interrupt and don't preach.

•Through "teachable moments"- in contrast to a formal lecture, use a variety of situations- television news, TV dramas, books, newspapers.

•Establish an ongoing conversation rather than giving a one-time speech.

•Remember that you set the example. Avoid contradictions between your words and your actions. And don't use illegal drugs, period!!

•Be creative! You and your child might act out various situations in which one person tries to pressure another to take a drug. Figure out two or three ways to handle each situation and talk about which works best.

•Exchange ideas with other parents.

How can I tell if a child is using drugs?

➤Identifying illegal drug use may help prevent further abuse. **Possible signs include:**

➤ Change in moods- more irritable, secretive, withdrawn, overly sensitive, inappropriately angry, and euphoric.

➤Less responsible- late coming home, late for school or class, dishonest.

➤Change friends or changing lifestyles- new interest, unexplained cash..

➤Physical deterioration- difficulty in concentration, loss of coordination, loss of weight, unhealthy appearance.

➤Refuses to talk or be around family.

Why do people use drugs?

Young people say they turn to alcohol and other drugs for one or more of these reasons:

▪To do what their friends are doing.

▪To escape pain in their lives.

▪To fit in, to take risks.

▪Boredom, for fun, curiosity.

What do we need to do as parents?

●Take a stand against illicit substance use in your family!!!!

What can we do to take a stand?

●Educate yourself about the facts surrounding alcohol and other drug use. You will lose credibility with your child if your information is not correct.

•Establish clear family rules against drug use and enforce them consistently.

What can we do to take a stand?

•Develop your parenting skills through seminars, networking with other parents, reading, counseling, and support groups.

•Work with other parents to set community standards - you don't raise a child alone.

•Volunteer at schools, youth centers, Boys & Girls Clubs, or other activities in your community.

Discussing Divorce

Discussing Divorce

Divorce is not an uncommon event in families. For many it is almost a normal stage in their family's life. Sometimes a divorce will take place while a child is enrolled in school.

Divorce can be a very stressful event for children, so some people wonder if it is better for parents to stay together "for the sake of the children." Researchers have not been able to agree whether it is always better to divorce or to stay together. They do agree that both choices can be hard on children. It can be confusing for children to deal with divorce. Divorce can be a sad event for the family, or it can be a relief. In any case, it can be hard for childcare providers to know how to respond.

Most parents who decide to divorce have taken some time to reach this decision. The children might know the divorce is coming, or it may be a surprise. The children are more likely to know the divorce is coming if they are older, if the parents talk to the children about problems, or if the parents have been fighting in front of the children. Even before the divorce happens, the child might be sad, angry, confused, or afraid about what is happening. The child might show those reactions in your childcare or school setting.

This section will give you some information on how divorce affects children of various ages and how to recognize when children are upset about something. You will get some tips on helping children through this time, some ideas about how to talk to parents, and some background on a few legal issues.

Childcare providers can help parents notice children's feelings.

All children are different. Some are bright and happy. Others are quiet and enjoy playing by themselves. Some argue and say what they think. Others are shy and careful. It takes only a few days for you to learn about each child's pace and personality, and how the child behaves. When they are upset, children may suddenly act very differently. They become "babyish," losing a skill that they had yesterday. For example, a child who was starting to walk may go back to crawling. An easy-going child might start getting angry or fearful. Changes like these could mean that the child is feeling stress. It could mean that there is a problem between the child's parents. But a change in the child's behavior is not always a sign that something is wrong with the marriage. Children may show behavior changes for many reasons. The parent may have changed work hours, or the child might not be feeling well. Children respond in similar ways to many different situations. It is important to check out what the real issue is. *Childcare can be a place where things do not change as much.* It is very important for children to feel safe and loved at times of stress. Researchers have found that it is best for the child to be close to at least one parent during a divorce. That is not always possible, though. Sometimes, when parents first start the divorce process, they are too angry or hurt to be able to help the child. At that time, childcare may be the only secure place for the child. You may be the familiar, comforting figure in the child's world—a world that is now confusing. The time spent in your childcare setting may be very important. You can provide some of the help that the parent cannot provide.

Childcare arrangements may need to change to help the parents in their new situation.

A divorce could cause major changes in the parents' schedules. Their childcare needs may change. You may have to work with both parents. You need to know which parent will pick up the child, and who will drop him off on what days. What if a parent has a crisis on the job while the child is in his or her custody? Will you offer flexible or extended times of childcare? Should you let the child go home with the other parent? You need to know who pays for childcare, when the child will be in which home, and whom to contact during an emergency. All of these issues are important. We will try to give you help with these questions in this section.

Children's Reactions to Divorce -- Ages and Stages

Children react to divorce differently at different ages. It is helpful for you as a childcare provider to know what thoughts and feelings to expect at different ages. This way you can change your behaviors to help children of different ages adjust to the divorce.

Toddlers

Toddlers might be able to understand some of the words that people use when they talk about divorce. But it is difficult for toddlers to really understand divorce. Toddlers live in the present. To prepare them for a divorce is difficult, because they cannot understand the future. But they do understand that changes are happening in their life. They know that one parent is not living at home. Toddlers might show they are unhappy or upset about these changes by crying often or becoming cranky and fussy. They can pout. Or they can become aggressive with a parent or other children in the childcare setting. They may have trouble sleeping and may throw temper tantrums. Children do not feel guilt until around 3 ½ or 4 years, so toddlers

probably will not blame themselves for their parents'
separation.

During a divorce everyone may be a bit confused.
The toddler can notice this confusion. He might also
notice that his parents pay him less attention, or that
schedules have been changed. Toddlers can also
start acting like younger children. A child who had
begun to walk may go back to crawling. Children's
feelings can also show some changes. They may
try to cling or cry when parents drop them off in
childcare. Children who were comfortable and easy-
going with you may now become cranky, anxious,
and quiet. On the other hand, some children may
also start staying close to adults rather than playing
out in the yard with other kids. Their moods may

change, swinging between fear and anger, or they may become shy and timid. They may also have nightmares and suck their thumbs. These are signs that the child is feeling upset.

Here are some things that parents can do to help toddlers during a time of divorce. You could share these suggestions with other parents who are worried about the changes that they notice in their children.

• Keep normal schedules and routines at home. Try not to change any more things than necessary.

• Reassure infants and toddlers. Let them know that you are still there. Use lots of hugs and loving words.

• Keep children's favorite toys, blankets, or stuffed animals close at hand. If you do not allow children to bring items from home to the childcare setting, look for special toys at childcare. Find something that the child can hold for a long time.

• Give children a little more time to say goodbye. Ask parents to spend more time when they drop the children off.

• Be patient. Allow children to be upset. Let children be babyish for a while. The more advanced behavior should return soon.

• Find out what the children know about the divorce.

•Parents talk about their plans for schedules and living situations.

Help the child understand what will change and what will not change.

• Do not change the rules just because of the divorce. Discipline as you always would. The child needs guidelines.

Preschool and early elementary children

Children from the age 3 to 10 will know that one parent no longer lives at home. Elementary school children begin to understand that divorce means that their parents will no longer be married and live together. They may understand that their parents no longer love each other. Children in this age group may blame themselves for the divorce. A child may think, "Mom and Dad are fighting because I was bad." Children in this stage have a better understanding than younger children of how their lives will be different because of the parents' divorce. They may worry about the changes in their daily lives. They may have nightmares. They may be sad because of the absence of one parent. Sometimes they may be angry with the parent who left. At other times, they may be angry with the parent who stayed. Preschoolers may be aggressive and angry toward one or both parents. Preschoolers and early elementary children also like to pretend. They might make up stories about how mom and dad are going to get back together.

What can childcare providers do for preschool and early elementary children?

- Tell children that they are not responsible for the divorce. You may need to say it many times.

- Explain who will take care of the children and what changes will happen.

- Talk with children about their thoughts and feelings; be sensitive to children's fears.

- Help both parents be involved in the childcare, if possible.

- Do not take sides. Help the child feel good about both parents as much as possible.

- Read books together about children and divorce.

- Gently remind children that the divorce is final and that parents will not get back together again.

Explaining Divorce to Children as a third party

It is difficult to know how to talk to children about divorce. However, research has shown that talking to children about the divorce is helpful for them. Explaining about divorce helps them to make some sense of what is happening in the family. By talking to children, adults can help them understand tension between parents, a parent moving out of the house, or the unhappiness and anger of a parent. It is common for children to think that somehow they are responsible for things going wrong. It can be reassuring to tell them that parents were having problems and that it was not the child's fault.

Children need some time to adjust to the idea of divorce. They may have many questions about what divorce means.

- Will they see the parents?

- Will they live in the same house or go to the same school?
- Will they see their friends?

- Who will take care of them?

- Can parents' divorce the children or stop loving them, too?

- Would the parents have stayed together if the children had been "good?"

Explaining the divorce to the children can give answers to some of these questions. The explanations can also help children with questions that they may not even know how to ask.

Remember that divorce is confusing for children. When you first talk with them, include only the most important and immediate issues. Children need to hear that their basic needs will be met. They need to hear that someone will still fix breakfast in the morning, read books with them, and tuck them in bed at night. Children also need to know that their relationship with BOTH parents will continue, if possible. This is why it is very important to have discussions with parents about what you can tell the children. You will need to ask parents whether the children will have contact with both parents. Find out from the parents what will be the same or different in the child's life now. This will help you decide what to tell the children.

Here are some suggestions that may help in explaining divorce to children:

- Talk with the parents before you talk with the children. Take the parent's lead.

- Give information that is consistent with what parents have already told the child.

- Keep the explanations simple.

- Keep the explanations appropriate to the child's age and development.

- Focus on the immediate concerns of the child.

- Avoid blaming either parent.

- Avoid talking about details. Use general statements. These statements can be very helpful:

- "Mom and Dad have decided they would be happier living in different homes."

- "Daddy and Mommy have decided not to live together in the same house."

- "Daddy and Mommy will not be married anymore. They will be divorced. I know you are sorry this has to be the way,

but Mommy and Daddy think this is best for everyone."

- It is best to avoid saying, "Daddy and Mommy don't love one another anymore." Children often hear that they are loved.

If parents talk about not loving each other anymore, a child may fear that he will also lose the parents' love if he misbehaves.

- Listen to the child's questions. Find out what she already knows. Take the lead from the child.

- Be prepared for children to ask the same questions again and again.
- Avoid giving false hopes that the parents may get back together.
- Keep telling the children that the divorce is not their fault.

<u>*What to explain and how*</u>

- ***Explain that children are not responsible for the divorce***

Tell children that the divorce is not their fault. Many children who are 4 or 5 or older believe that the divorce is the result of something that they did. For example, some children may think that parents are divorcing because the child misbehaved or received bad grades in school. Children need to be told again and again that they are not responsible for the divorce.

- ***Explain that the divorce is permanent***

Make it very clear to children that the parents will not be getting back together. Children need to hear that they cannot rescue or restore the marriage. At some ages, children may also make up stories about their parents getting back together. It is okay to pretend, but explain that the parents are really separated. This can help the children move on and accept other changes that may come into their lives.

• *Explain that their parents love them, and there parents' love for them will not change*

Help children understand that the love shared between a parent and a child is special. It is different from the love shared between a husband and wife. Husbands and wives might get divorced, but parents are always parents. Children need to know that the love parents have for them will last.

- ***Help children deal with the balancing act of relating to two divorced parents***

Help children understand that it will be confusing to deal with their two parents. It may be hard to love both of them at once when the parents don't love each other. Tell children that it's OK to love both Mom and Dad. Children should not feel they have to take sides or worry about losing the love of either parent. After a divorce, children's loyalty may become split. They may feel caught between the parents. Though the parents may never ask a child to take sides, children can still feel they have to choose one parent over the other. Many children take a long time to work through feelings of split loyalty. This is a normal process of children adjusting to their parents' divorce. As a childcare provider, you may be able to help the child deal with these issues. You may say, "Sometimes you may feel guilty for missing Dad while you are staying with Mom. Sometimes you may feel you have to choose whether you love Mom more or Dad more. It's OK to feel all these confused feelings and thoughts. Many children feel that way when their parents get divorced."

• *Give children a chance to express their feelings, and name the different feelings they have*

Sometimes younger children do not understand what they are feeling. You can help them learn about feelings by reading books to them about divorce. You can read books about feelings, too. You also can do activities that will help children understand feelings.

• *Explain that they are not alone in the way they feel*

Children can feel that they are the only ones who have these troubles. They may feel that their family is the only one that has ever gone through divorce. You can help children learn that divorce happens in many families. This can help the children feel less alone. If you have divorce in your family, you could share how you feel about it. For example, you may say, "I'm sorry that this is so sad for you. I can understand. I feel sad, too. I remember when my parents divorced..." Help children understand that they are not the only ones feeling sad or angry or relieved. You may help the child understand the parents by saying, "Mom and Dad are probably sad about the divorce too. I am sure they are sorry this had to happen to you. They may wish that your family did not have to separate just like you do. How do you think they are feeling? What do you think makes them happy and what makes them sad about the divorce?" This can teach children that everyone has some of the same feelings. It is OK to have feelings and express them to others.

• *Help children understand that their feelings may be different from the parents' or siblings' feelings*

Let children know that members of the family may not always share the same feelings about the divorce. Explain to the children that it's all right to feel differently from the parents and from brothers and sisters. A child may not understand why Mom or Dad is relieved about the divorce while the child is sad and hurt. Explain to the child that people have different feelings and that feelings are neither right nor wrong. For example, you could say, "I know you are hurt that Daddy left home. But he and Mom may have been unhappy for a long time. This divorce may be a relief for them. But it is OK for you to be sad." Tell them that feelings may be different on different days, too.

• *Check with the children often about their fears and concerns*

Watch for signs that show how the children are feeling. Let them talk about their fears, concerns, and feelings about the divorce or about what is happening at home now. Give children time to think about the divorce and the changes it may have brought about. Don't expect to have only one big discussion. Talk as many times as the issue may come up. Children will want to talk about different issues as time goes on. Take children's questions and concerns seriously and LISTEN to what they say. As one older child said, "this is going to affect the rest of my life and I don't know if they just don't realize that, or don't care, or what, but I don't feel like I'm being heard." Children need to know that adults (caregivers, parents, and concerned others) want to help them deal with the divorce and are concerned about how the divorce is affecting them.

Explaining divorce to other children as childcare provider or third party

As a provider or third party, you may need to explain the divorce of one child's parents to other children in your care or close to your family. These children may wonder why Juan lives with his father on the weekend and with his mother during the weekdays. They may ask questions about why Jenny's father never comes to the childcare to pick her up, or what Jenny means when she says that her parents are divorced. You can help them understand by using simple statements. The other children do not need to know details, but they do need some information. This will also make it easier for the child in the divorcing family. She will not need to explain if you take care of it.

As a childcare provider or third party, you can help children in your setting understand divorce and treat the children whose parents have divorced in a kind way. Sometimes the other children may ask the child in the divorcing family many questions. Sometimes they are curious. Other times they may make fun of the child or tease her. These reactions can make the child from the divorced family feel embarrassed, hurt, or ashamed. It is important to watch for these reactions and to try to avoid them from the beginning. Give a simple explanation to the children about divorce. Talk about it in a natural tone of voice. You can make divorce a normal thing.

When children have answers, they will usually go on to other topics and stop questioning a specific child.

There are some words that you could use that will fit almost all divorce situations. You could say, "Jason's Mom and Dad were not happy living together. They have decided that it is best if they live in separate houses. Adults go through what they call a divorce when they decide to live separately like this and are not married any more. Even though Jason's Mom and Dad are not married, they love Jason very much, and they will always be his Mom and Dad."

Sometimes a childcare setting will include more than one child whose parents have divorced. If that is true in your childcare, those other children can be very helpful. They can show that divorce does not need to be a secret, and they can help the child realize that she is not alone. The children may help each other by sharing their experiences.

Some children may be afraid that their own parents will also divorce. This may be difficult to answer. You may not know if there are problems in the families. But you may be able to help the children with that question. You can answer, "Sometimes when parents are not getting along together, they decide to divorce. But not all parents make this decision. Most parents stay together, even though they might argue sometimes. Others may divorce. But even if they decide to divorce, both parents will love their children." You can also tell the children to ask their parents this question. Parents are in the best position to reassure the child that they are not getting a divorce. It may be helpful to let parents know if children ask about whether their parents will divorce. You can tell them you asked the child to talk to them. This way they can be prepared with an answer for their child.

Gang Section

Four Reasons Why Kids Join Gangs

1. **Identity or Recognition**- being a part of a gang allows the members to achieve a level of status the feel they cannot achieve outside of the gang's culture.

2. **Protection**- Kids join the gang because they live in a gang area and are subject to violent by rival gangs. Kids join in an attempt to obtain safety from this violence.

3. **Fellowship and Brotherhood**- The gang functions as an extension of, or substitute for, the family and may provide companionship lacking in the home environment.

4. **Intimidation**- Some members may be forced into joining by peer groups. Intimidation

techniques range from extorting lunch money to physical assault.

How can I tell if my child is in a gang?

Be aware of the friends with whom your child associates. What kind of clothing does your child wear? Is a particular color or piece of clothing always part of what he or she wears? Does he or she have graffiti on their school book covers?

Are gangs mainly comprised of disadvantaged youths?

Gang members can come from virtually every socio-economic level in the community. They can be from the homes of the very rich to the homes of the very poor.

Are gangs racially segregated?

There are gangs that are comprised of one race exclusively and there are gangs that are integrated. Most cities that have gangs have gangs that are exclusively Black, exclusively Hispanic, exclusively White and exclusively Asian. There are also racially mixed gangs.

Are gang members armed? What type of weapons do they carry?

Gang members are sometimes armed. They carry an assortment of weapons ranging from sticks and baseball bats to firearms.

How do kids join gangs?

Kids normally join a street gang by either committing a crime or by being "jumped in". "Jumped in" is an initiation which involves other gang members beating the perspective members as a test of his or her courage and fighting ability.

What is the description of a gang member?

> ➢ Usually male

> ➢ School dropout or truant; poor student who does not like school and who does not adapt well to school.

> ➢ Negative contact with law enforcement.

> ➢ Does not receive adequate family attention.

> ➢ Victim of abuse or neglect, and/or parental brutality

> ➢ Economically and/or socially deprived backgrounds.

> ➢ Negative role models.

> ➢ Very streetwise.

> ➢ Antisocial, aggressive, and hostile.

Self- Esteem Section

Self- Esteem- is the ability to feel good about ourselves whether or not we are always. Successful it is a feeling of satisfaction we experience after our needs are met.

Critical Question asked by Parents

1. How do I build my child's self esteem at home?

We as parents can help build our children's self-esteem by telling them positive things about themselves. Additionally, we must praise them for good decisions, small deeds and great initiatives. Lastly, parents must acknowledge their child's potential. If a parent does not speak of the child's unlimited possibilities, their child may become susceptible to negative peer feedback. Henceforth, sending them into an unsuspecting path of poor decisions and negative consequences. As parents, it is our responsibility to assist our children in feeling good about themselves.

2. How do I communicate with my child?
We can communicate with our children if we respect them first. Most children will rebel out of anger if we don't respect them. It is essential to listen to the concerns of our children because they have issues that must be addressed. In turn, children will learn the principal of respect and will display this virtue through their actions toward you as well as others. Furthermore, children learn what they are taught. If they are not in an environment where respect is essential, their immediate response to respect or being ask to give respect will be tough.

3. How do I get my child to talk to me?
If children trust our judgment they will talk to us. The first lie we tell as parents is "You can talk to me about anything," and the first time they ask about sex or drugs we erupt in an uncontrollable fit of anger or become mute

and unable to communicate effectively. Unfortunately, millions of parents result to threatening their children with physical violence or unreasonable and meaningless punishments when their child attempts to talk with them. This negative reaction will ensure that they will never approach or confide in you again. Therefore, the most important thing we need to do is make our children feel comfortable in talking to us. Moreover, we need to ask our children how they feel about all social and personal issues that may arise. However, we can't ignore, over react or minimize their answers and opinions.

4. Will this advice work if I am a single parent?
Yes, this book will help you if you are a single parent. It's evident that our society is engaged with single parents. Henceforth, this parenting book was created for everyone; it isn't limited to any race, gender, or religion.

And single parents are encouraged to use this book to help raise their children. Understandable, single parents have fewer hours to offer their children…..BUT…. it can be done. It is important to stress that single parents should utilize ALL of the resources that are available to them (I. e. church, social service organizations, community centers and mentoring programs). Most of these resources are free and will assist you in your endeavors to guiding, nurturing and protect your child/children.

5. What does communication have to do with building self-esteem?
Communication is the key to success in any relationship. It's no different in building the self-esteem of our children. When we are able to talk with our children and tell them we love them: it helps build their self-esteem.

Therefore, that is why it is imperative to compliment our children on how they look and how smart they are. If we plant a positive self-image seed in our children's mind: the harvest will be high levels of self-esteem throughout their life.

Resolving Conflict Section

<u>Resolving Conflict Section</u>

The next important phase of development within our children is being able to resolve conflict without violence and confrontation. Unfortunately, our children often allow anger to control them when a conflict arises. Children will naturally lash out if they are annoyed or openly criticized by friends or family. A small conflict can affect a relationship forever if it isn't resolved properly.

When there is a conflict in the home between siblings or parents and children, below is a list of things we <u>SHOULD NOT do:</u>

1. not listen	6. Threats
2. name calling	7. hitting
3. blaming	8. making excuses
4. Not taking responsibility	9. insults
5. bringing up the past	10. cursing

The list of things we SHOULD do if the conflict is between parents and children:
1. Parents pray for wisdom to help you resolve the conflict.
2. Tell your children you love them and let your actions resemble your words.
3. Ensure your children that most issues can be worked out.
4. Recognize what the problem is.
5. Attack the problem and not your children.

6. Listen to our children with ears of love and not anger.
7. Care about our children's feelings.
8. Be responsible for a positive outcome to the conflict.

Most siblings' conflict revolves around someone wanting something or going first at a game or activity. We must teach our children the following strategies to resolve the conflict on their own.

<u>Six Strategies for Resolving Conflict our kids can use</u>

<u>Take</u> turns and everybody gets a chance.

<u>Share</u> what ever it is and they will understand that feelings are more important than things.

<u>Compromise</u> and both sibilings' give up something to get something.

<u>Apologize-</u> Teach them that when they apologize it doesn't mean that they are wrong. It means you are apologizing about the disagreement.

<u>Chance</u> let them flip a coin to decide who goes first or plays first.

<u>Parent Resolution</u> you resolve the situation via removing the object away from both siblings or making a final decision that ends the problem.

Using the above strategies for resolving conflict will help you and your children attain that level of peace in the above strategies for resolving conflict will help you and your children attain that level of peace in the home we all are searching for. If we teach our children and remember ourselves that we love each other, we will always attempt to solve our conflicts positively.

Problem:

Two siblings want to play with a toy. The oldest sibling will want it first. The younger sibling will want it just because the older sibling has it.

Solution:

First, we as parents have to instruct our children to take turns with the toy, share the toy or have the toy taken away as a result of not being willing to resolve this conflict.

Decision Making Section

<u>Decision Making Section</u>

Unfortunately, our children can't be around us all day, so we have to trust their decisions when they are away. The decisions of our children may affect their lives forever. We have to help our children identify the consequences that must be considered.

We as parents have all been in a situation where we were approach to participate in "unproductive or dangerous" activities. And because we all want to be accepted and have friends sometimes we gave in and sometimes we took a stance to do what was right. However, it is essential to remember and relate to this feeling in order to help our children.

<u>Rule #1- Make It Known That You Are Not Perfect</u>

Our children embrace the truth. Admitting that you are not perfect does not require ANY parent to reveal DETAILS of their past indiscretion….it simply keeps the lines of communication open for everyone. This section of the booklet was created to introduce a model for our parents and children to follow when making a decision.

Eight Step Decision Making Model

Step- 1   Recognize what the situation is.

Step-2   Who is involved in the situation.

Step-3   What are the two choices in the situation.

Step-4   What are the positive consequences of choice one.

Step-5   What are the negative consequences of choice one.

Step-6   What are the positive consequences of choice two.

Step-7   What are the negative consequences of choice two.

Step-8   After attempting to think through all of the previous steps then our children can make an informed decision.

If our children use part of the eight steps it will help them

make better decisions. We need to encourage our

children to think before they make decisions.

Problem:

You suspect your child of using drugs. The first step is to identify the symptoms. Laziness, mood swings, change in eating habits, and change in peer group.

Step-2 Consider their friends behavior that they associate with on a daily basis.

Step-3 The two choices in this situation are:

- Choice #1 searches your child's room while they aren't home for drugs.

- Choice #2 ask your child directly if they are doing drugs.

Step-4 The positive consequences of searching your child's room is you find the drugs and you can get your child help.

Step-5 The negative consequence of searching your child's room is you don't find anything. Immediately you will feel guilty about snooping around in their room.

Step-6 The positive consequences of asking your child directly if they are using drugs is they could tell you the truth and the answer is no.

Step-7 The negative consequences of asking your child directly if they are using drugs. They could lie or say yes and continue to use drugs with their friends if you do not.

Step-8 Make a decision.

Social Media

Social media has seemingly taken over our online lives. From political discussions to fantastic getaways, to global collaboration, most people who are active online participate in social media. As individuals on their way into adulthood, teens have become a vibrant and active online community. However, as a responsible parent it can oftentimes seem overwhelming to keep up with your teens and their online presence.

We at The Caring Corner have compiled bits of advice that we think can help you navigate parenting the online teen. Don't forget that parents who are involved in their teen's offline lives, will find it easier to facilitate an active dialogue.

In your quest to prepare your child for life as an adult and active member of society, they need to know best online practices – and it is your job to help teach them. Sexually explicit and other inappropriate content, bullying, and copyright infringement are all some of the pitfalls of teens social media use. Just like in the real world, there is no foolproof way to guarantee your child won't experience some of the negative aspects social media. However, you can equip them with the tools to be smart.

Want to raise teens who think before they post, speak up when someone else is being harmful, and protect their privacy? Consider these five tips:

1) **Communication is key!**
Teens can often be impulsive and short sighted. An open dialogue with your teen about what it means to be online

will help foster a sense of trust so you can help guide them. Be sure to remind them that what they post online is there forever. Words, images and videos posted there can be used by anyone at any time. This means law enforcement, future employers, their extended family, and most importantly YOU can see everything they put there – password protected or not.

Being able to talk to them about what it means to have "good judgment" is important for their lives on and off line. You can start the conversation by talking a bit about your own use. This also lets them know that you know how it works.

2) **Know what you're talking about!**
As an active parent, there is no better way to understand what your kids are doing online than to use what they use. Get a Facebook account. Join Twitter. Stay current. Yes – it can be exhausting, but being engaged in the same sites your kids are using means that you have a full understanding of their participation. We've identified some further reading below that will help you in this quest.

3) **Get in control!**
The biggest thing you can do to keep your teens safe online. There are several products on the market that allow you to monitor your teen's use. It's easy to delete a browsing history – however many of the products available allow you to silently track your teen's use of the computer. The first video below details some specific ways you can be a better monitor. You should know that

it is easy to set up dummy accounts online, so "friending" your teen on Facebook, sharing passwords, etc only works so far. It's up to you as a parent to decide how much you trust your teen's activity online. However, know that as a parent, it's best practice to snoop in on their online activity.

4) Don't forget that their phone is also a gateway to the internet.

Did you know that most teens access popular sites like Facebook and Instagram from their phone and rarely even go to them from a computer? Be mindful that an inappropriate image captured on a phone can be easily and instantly posted anywhere online. With sexting on the rise, this can lead to images finding their way into the public, online sphere. Again, teens can be short sighted and impulsive. Be sure to talk to them about keeping best practices with their phone as well, and remember to manage their data usage.

5) Manage their time spent with "screens."

Make sure you and your kids spend time off of their various devices. Go for a walk. Play a board game. Cook together. They don't want to do that with you? Keep them active in other extracurricular activities and sports. The increase of sedentary lives has had a major impact on the health of youth. Encourage and foster a culture of activity in your home so that your teens see the benefits.

As with anything, keeping your teens safe yet worldly means that you'll have to actively participate in their lives. It means having open dialogue with them so that there is trust on both sides.

Need more info? Glossary of popular social media sites for teens:

Facebook – You probably already know this one. However, remember that most teens access this site by their phone.

Twitter – Users get 140 characters to broadcast their thoughts around the globe. Twitter has made it easy to keep up with current events, shout out your favorite celebrity, and find humor. However, due to the fast-pace nature of Twitter, teens may think their words go unnoticed.

Instagram – Here, people post pictures from their phone. Their "followers" are instantly updated with these pictures, and oftentimes their geolocation. It's like twitter, but for pictures only. People often link their Instagram accounts to their other social media networks, so what they post travels instantly.

Tumblr – This is an easy blog site for people looking to quickly get their thoughts online. It carries the same pitfalls as site like Facebook – only – your posts are not limited to your friends. They are posted and reblogged and favorited by anyone who also has a Tumblr account.

YouTube – We've probably all seen a viral video or two. However, remember that anyone can easily post to YouTube, and your kids may want to emulate what they see others posting.

IM - Or, Instant Messaging. You'll want to especially watch usage here because it is seemingly private. However, teens must remember that anything shared in a conversation can be easily copied and pasted elsewhere online.

Reddit – Reddit is a social website that allows its users to share links to content on the internet and post comments about the links. This enables not only the sharing of content (photographs, videos, websites, and so on) but also the discussion of said content. It is a bastion of forums and commentary. This site isn't as popular as Facebook, however you should know that this where many people go to say what they think won't be seen by the masses (ie parents). This is a false sense of security. For example, Anderson Cooper recently did an expose on the "jailbait." Section on this site. You'll want to closely monitor usage of this site.

iChan – in some ways this site is similar to Reddit… only it's much easier to find pornographic materials here. You're supposed to be over 18 to use it, but that's easy to get around.

If you think you're hip to your children's online social habits because you know all about Facebook and Twitter, and the other sites previously mentioned, you've got it all wrong. Tweens and teens are increasingly leaving these sites in favor of new apps that offer richer features and a safe haven from watchful parents.

For some parents, this might be more of a trick than a treat because of the greater potential for cyberbullying, online harassment and other inappropriate activity, which can fly under the radar if you're not actively monitoring these newer sites. In fact, one of the reasons why teens are moving away from Facebook specifically toward other smaller, more niche sites, is precisely because "my mom doesn't have that" -- according to a recent Pew study. This may be easy to understand, since the study found that 70% of teens have been friended on Facebook by their parents.

As more parents embrace Facebook, they're driving teens and tweens away as they look for other, more secretive venues that won't be subjected to the same level of parental scrutiny. For parents, this creates a tricky situation: How can you keep track of your kids' online activity when you don't even know what sites they're using and it's hard to keep up with all the startup apps that roll out?

Here are eight scary social networking sites your teen or tween may be using:

1. **Creepy** - Did you know that with just a Twitter or Facebook ID, you can track someone's every move and find their exact current location? Creepy does just that -- it allows anyone with access to another person's online photos to pull sensitive geotag location data, allowing them to pinpoint where the photo was taken. Just provide Creepy with the needed username and it will retrieve all the locations the user has posted photos from.

2. **Ask.fm** - This Latvia-based social networking website allows users to ask other users questions, with the option of anonymity. It's this anonymity and

unmoderated Q&A forum that has been criticized by many parents and anti-bullying organizations. As an example, questions like "Why are you a loser?" "Why are you ugly?" etc. are common on the site. Ask.fm is not well-known by many adults, but it has been associated with instances of cyberbullying in teens and a series of bullying-relatedsuicides.

3.   **Vine** - While this mobile app can be used to post short videos, some teens are using the app to videotape others without their knowledge or using the app to mock or harass other kids.

4.   **Snapchat** - Widely known as the "sexting app," Snapchat allows users to take photos, record videos, add text and drawings and send them to a controlled list of followers. The followers can only view the photos for a short period of time, after which SnapChat supposedly destroys them. However, many users get around this 'self-destructing' feature by taking screen shots of the photos. This app has been associated with numerous sexting cases among teens that led to harassment.

5.   **KiK** - An instant messenger service designed for use on smartphones. This is another app that has been widely associated with sexting.

6.   **Pheed** - Some have called this the next big social app for teens, with 81% of its user base between 14-25 years old. One the site's more popular features is the ability for teens to livestream what they're doing at any given moment. It's yet another social media platform that allows for the sharing of all sorts of content, including text, photos, videos and audio.

7.   **Qooh.me** - This is another social media site that allows teens to ask other users anonymous questions. This type of open access site can pose problems for teens/tweens, as users do not have to login to ask questions, there is no online moderator to check for disturbing content and adult profiles are mixed in with those of teens and children.

8.   **Oovoo** - A startup video chat and instant messaging application that is similar to Skype and Apple's Facetime. While this site blocks those under 13 from registering, youngsters need only lie about their age to set up an account.

It is important for parents to talk openly with their kids about these apps and the risks they carry. Another option is to restrict your child's access to these apps -- both the iPhone and Android devices have parental settings that you can use to block certain types of activity. For parents who want to track their kids, there are activity monitors.

- **Instagram** is another well known app that it seems everyone is on (though being bought by Facebook didn't improve its cachet). Though it's a picture-posting forum, the level of social engagement it provides, like Tumblr, may surprise those who haven't used it. Who follows who, who liked what, who faked #nofilter, it's definitely fertile ground for gossip. And picture feeds full of selfies and favorite places may be open for the public to view, by oversight or on purpose — parents will have to decide whether it's creepy or innocuous. Instagram lets users follow one another and share pictures - but a fair amount of socializing gets done, too.

- **Pheed** is the latest thing to come along, merging the mixed-media feed of Tumblr with the instantaneous sharing of Kik and video chatting. Users can put statuses, photos, videos, audio and even live broadcasts — and you can even charge for people to access your "pheed," if you think they'll pay. Teens have jumped onto it, following the pheeds of celebrities, DJs and friends.

- A kid may be using one, some, or all of these apps. It's important to remember that they're not intrinsically bad in any way. But the potential for abuse is always there, especially when kids have a public-facing profile that can be viewed and contacted by anyone on the Internet. Being aware of the apps and services your kids are using — even if they'd rather you didn't know — is an increasingly important part of smart parenting.

Bullying

What Parents Can Do

Advice for Parents and Adults About How To Deal With Bullying

A big, tough kid stops a smaller kid on his way to school and threatens to hurt him unless he hands over his homework. The popular girls at school won't let anyone sit at their lunch table except their friends. These two bullying scenarios and others happen more often than most adults realize. <u>Seventy-four percent</u> of eight to 11-year-olds say teasing and bullying happen at their school. But what exactly is bullying?

Bullying is

- Fighting, threatening, name-calling, teasing, or excluding someone repeatedly and over time
- An imbalance of power, such as size or popularity
- Physical, social, and emotional harm
- Hurting another person to get something

Many parents don't think that bullying is as big a problem as bringing a weapon to school or drug use but its effects can be severe and long lasting. Every day, nearly 160,000 children miss school because they are scared of bullying, according to the <u>National Education Association</u>. Bullying doesn't only negatively affect its victims, but also the bullies themselves.

Kids who are bullied are more likely to

- Do poorly in school
- Have low self-esteem
- Be depressed

- Turn to violent behavior to protect themselves or get revenge on their bullies

Kids who bully are more likely to

- Do poorly in school
- Smoke and drink alcohol
- Commit crimes in the future

Parents can play a central role to preventing bullying and stopping it when it happens. Here are a few things you can do.

- Teach kids to solve problems without using violence and praise them when they do.
- Give children positive feedback when they behave well to help their build self-esteem. Help give them the self-confidence to stand up for what they believe in.
- Ask your children about their day and listen to them talk about school, social events, their classmates, and any problems they have.
- Take bullying seriously. Many kids are embarrassed to say they have been bullied. You may only have one chance to step in and help.
- If you see any bullying, stop it right away, even if your child is the one doing the bullying.
- Encourage your child to help others who need it.
- Don't bully your children or bully others in front of them. Many times kids who are bullied at home react by bullying other kids. If your children see you hit,

ridicule, or gossip about someone else, they are also more likely to do so themselves.

- Support bully prevention programs in your child's school. If your school doesn't have one, consider starting one with other parents, teachers, and concerned adults.

When Your Child Is Bullied

Many kids are embarrassed to be bullied and may not tell their parents or another adult right away. If your child comes to you and asks for help with a bully, take it seriously. Many times, if kids aren't taken seriously the first time they ask for help, they don't ask again.

Even if your child doesn't turn to you for help, you can watch for these warning signs that he or she is being bullied. Kids who are bullied often experience

- Withdrawal
- A loss of friends
- A drop in grades
- A loss of interest in activities he or she previously enjoyed
- Torn clothing
- Bruises
- A need for extra money or supplies

If you think your child is being bullied or if your child has told you that he or she is being bullied, you can help. Parents are often the best resource to build a child's self-confidence and teach him or her how to best solve problems. Here are a few ways you can help

- Talk to your child's teacher about it instead of confronting the bully's parents. If the teacher doesn't act to stop the bullying, talk to the principal.
- Teach your child nonviolent ways to deal with bullies, like walking away, playing with friends, or talking it out.
- Help your child act with self-confidence. With him or her, practice walking upright, looking people in the eye, and speaking clearly.
- Don't encourage your child to fight. This could lead to him or her getting hurt, getting in trouble, and beginning more serious problems with the bully.
- Involve your child in activities outside of school. This way he or she can make friends in a different social circle.

Some children seem to be bullied all the time, while others rarely get picked on. Why do some kids seem to attract all of the bullies? Kids who are bullied often

- Are different from other kids, whether by size, race, sexually, or have different interests
- Seem weak, either physically or emotionally
- Are insecure
- Want approval
- Won't tell on their bullies

When Your Child Is a Bully

It's hard for any parent to believe that their child is a bully, but sometimes it happens. But just because your child bullies doesn't mean that he or she will bully forever. Parents are one of the best resources to help their child stop bullying and start interacting positively with their classmates.

Your child may bully if, he or she

- Lacks empathy and doesn't sympathize with others
- Values aggression
- Likes to be in charge
- Is an arrogant winner and a sore loser
- Often fights often with brothers and sisters
- Is impulsive

What you can do to stop your child from bullying

- Take it seriously. Don't treat bullying as a passing phase. Even if you're not worried about long-lasting effects on your child, another child is being hurt.

- Talk to your child to find out why he or she is bullying. Often, children bully when they feel sad, angry, lonely, or insecure and many times major changes at home or school may bring on these feelings.

- Help build empathy for others and talk to your child about how it feels to be bullied.

- Ask a teacher or a school counselor if your child is facing any problems at school, such as if your child is struggling with a particular subject or has difficulty making friends. Ask them for advice on how you and your child can work through the problem.

- Ask yourself if someone at home is bullying your child. Often, kids who bully are bullied themselves by a parent, family member, or another adult.

Sexting

1. Sexting is defined by the U.S. court system as "an act of sending sexually explicit materials through mobile phones." The messages may be text, photo, or video.

2. 22 percent of high-school age teens (ages 14 to 17) and 33 percent of college-age students (ages 18 to 24) have been involved in a form of nude sexting.

3. Sending or receiving a sexually suggestive text or image under the age of 18 is considered child pornography and can result in criminal charges.

4. Among 14-to-24 –years-old who admit to sexting, 29 percent send these messages to people they have never met, but know from the Internet.

5. Sending semi-nude or nude photos is more common among teen's girls. 22 percent girls report sending images of the nature, while only 18 percent of same-age boys have.

6. Nearly 40 percent of all teenagers have posted or sent sexually suggestive messages, but this practice is more common among boys than girls.

7. While nearly 70 percent of teen boys and girls who sext do so with their girlfriend and boyfriend, 61 percent of all sexters who have sent nude images that they were pressured to do it at least once.

8. Who will see your sext? 17 percent of sexters share the messages they receive with others, and 55 percent of those share them with more than one person.

9. Teenage girls a few reasons for sexting: 40 percent do it as a joke, 34 percent do it to feel sexy, and 12 percent feel pressured to do it.

10. In the U.S., 8 states have enacted bills to protect minors form sexting, and an additional 14 states have proposed bill to legislation.

11. 11 percent of teen girls ages 13 to 16 have been involved with sending or recording inappropriate pictures and or videos.

Goal Setting Section

Goal Setting Section

The next section of this book is on Goal Setting. We have a responsibility to our children to encourage them to set goals. We must also inform them that there are two types of goals short and long-term goals.

Types of Goals

Short Term Goals- are goals that you plan on reaching within a month or less.

Long Term Goals- are goals that you plan on reaching within the next few months or even years.

The importance of encouraging our children to set goals in their life is crucial to their success. Children who do not have goals eventually lack purpose in their lives and may never develop their true talents and abilities.

Now that we have addressed the different types of goals, the next step is to address how to set goals. There are five steps that will help you teach your children how to set goals.

Five Steps to Goal Setting

<u>Step-1</u>   Define what you really want to do.

<u>Step-2</u>   Decide what steps you must take to achieve

the goal.

<u>Step-3</u>   Think of what obstacles could get in the way
of you achieving your goal.

<u>Step-4</u>   Think of ways of overcoming your possible

obstacles.

<u>Step-5</u>   Set a deadline for each of your goals.

If you have children between the ages of 5 and 10 you need to consult with your children and write down the goals for them. Children between the ages of 11 to 19 should write down their goals and assist them in remaining realistic.

Once you have helped your children set some realistic goals for their life. We as parents also must teach them the three keys to reaching their goals.

Keys to Reaching Goals

Key #1 Self Discipline- you must be willing to focus and work on your goal whether you feel like it or not daily.

Key #2 Commitment- you must be willing to work towards attaining your goal on a consistent basis.

Key #3 Sacrifice- you may have to give up something like your time or your focus to get your goal.

When these three elements are applied and practiced our children ca reach any realistic goal.

Goal Setting Example

Step-1 The goal is to attend college.

Step-2 Outline the steps to completing high school and admission to college. For example, the SAT test, ACT test, and reviewing family financial status in order to determine whether student loans or federal grants will apply.

Step-3 Discuss the obstacles (i.e. Current grades and attitude toward school)

Step-4 Discuss how to improve current grades and attitudes about school. If family financial status is our obstacle set up a meeting with school guidance counselor in order to explore all alternatives.

Step-5 Set deadlines for the following:

Speaking with guidance counselor

Taking college level entrance exams.

Completing financial aid forms.

Completing applications to colleges of child's choice.

Goal Setting Activities for Home
Worksheet #1

Short Term Goals

Goals for the week:

1.____

____

2.____

____

3.____

____

Possible obstacles that could interfere with me reaching my goals:

1.__________________________________

2.__________________________________

3.__________________________________

Ways that I can overcome the possible obstacles:

1.__________________________________

2.__________________________________

3.__________________________________

Deadline for reaching these goals:
Dates:
1.___________ **2.**_____________ **3.**____________

Goal Setting Worksheet #2

Goals for the month:

1._______________________________

2._______________________________

3._______________________________

4._______________________________

5._______________________________

Possible obstacles that could interfere with me reaching my goals:

1._______________________________

2._______________________________

3._______________________________

4._______________________________

5._______________________________

Ways that I can overcome the possible obstacles:

1._______________________________

2._______________________________

3._______________________________

4._______________________________

5._______________________________

Deadline for reaching goals:

Dates: 1. _______ 2._______ 3._______

Goal Setting Worksheet #3

Long Term Goals

Goals for the year:

1.___________________________________
2.___________________________________
3.___________________________________
4.___________________________________
5.___________________________________

Possible obstacles that could interfere with me reaching my goals:

1.___________________________________
2.___________________________________
3.___________________________________
4.___________________________________
5.___________________________________

Ways that I can overcome the possible obstacles:

1._________________________________
2._________________________________
3._________________________________
4._________________________________
5._________________________________

Deadline for reaching goals:
Dates:

1._____   2.______   3._____   4.______
    5.______

Goals Worksheet # 4

Long Term Goals

Goals to be reached within the next five years:

1.______________________________
2.______________________________
3.______________________________
4.______________________________
5.______________________________

Possible obstacles that could interfere with me reaching my goals:

1.______________________________
2.______________________________
3.______________________________
4.______________________________
5.______________________________

Ways that I can overcome possible obstacles:

1.__________________________
2.__________________________
3.__________________________
4.__________________________
5.__________________________

Deadline for reaching goals:
Dates:

1._____   2._____   3._____   4._____
        5._____

Goals Worksheet #5

Evaluation of Goals

1. Did I reach all of my goal(s)? yes____ or no____

1. Why?

2. What could I change to achieve my goal(s) next time?

____

____

____

Self Esteem
Building Activities

Self Esteem Building Activities for the Home
Worksheet #1

A. Make a list of your strengths:

1.______________________________

2.______________________________

3.______________________________

4.______________________________

5.______________________________

B. Make a list of your weaknesses:

1.______________________________

2.______________________________

3.______________________________

4.______________________________

5.______________________________

C. How can you improve on your weaknesses ?

1.______________________________

2.______________________________

3.______________________________

4.______________________________

5.______________________________

Worksheet # 2

A. Write about the happiest day of your life:

____

____

____

____

____

____

____

____

____

____

____

B. Write about the saddest day of your life:

____

____

____

____

____

____

____

____

____

____

____

____

Worksheet #3

Create a poem about things that make you happy:

____

____

____

____

____

____

____

____

____

____

____

Create a poem about your family and friends:

Worksheet #4

List five qualities a friend should possess:

1.
2.
3.
4.
5.

Write the names of the family members you live with:

1.
2.
3.
4.
5.
6.
7.

List one talent or skill possessed by each family member named above:

1.______________________________________

2.______________________________________

3.______________________________________

4.______________________________________

5.______________________________________

6.______________________________________

7.______________________________________

<u>Worksheet # 5</u>

List the rules your family has that everyone is expected to follow:

1.________________________________

2.________________________________

3.________________________________

4.________________________________

5.________________________________

6.________________________________

7.________________________________

8.________________________________

9.________________________________

10._______________________________

<u>Worksheet #6</u>

Write a thank you letter to a family member that did something special for you lately:

Worksheet #7

Name_______________

1. I am somebody who likes
to___________________________

____

_______________.

2. My hobbies are ___________________.

3. One thing that makes me feel good is
   when my mom

____

4.One thing that makes me feel good is
when my dad

____

____

5. I have wonderful friends, but my best
friend is:_______________.

6. My favorite foods are :

____

____

____

**7. I enjoy spending time with my
grandparents because
they**_______________________________

____

____

Worksheet # 8

List fifteen things you love to do:

1. _______________________________
2. _______________________________
3. _______________________________
4. _______________________________
5. _______________________________
6. _______________________________
7. _______________________________
8. _______________________________
9. _______________________________
10. _______________________________
11. _______________________________
12. _______________________________
13. _______________________________
14. _______________________________
15. _______________________________

Worksheet # 9

Name:_____________________

Date:_______________

How I feel about myself and my family

My good qualities are:

1.______________________________
2.______________________________
3.______________________________

My dad's good qualities are:

1.______________________________
2.______________________________
3.______________________________

My mom's qualities are:

1.______________________________
2.______________________________
3.______________________________

<u>**Synopsis**</u>

In short, parenting is life's most tedious but rewarding task we have been bestowed. As parents, we are aware of numerous external issues and pressures that can influence and affect our children. However, the primary morals, values and virtues must be taught in the home. Parents have lasting and undeniable influence in the lives of their children and the job of parenting our children can never be taken lightly. Through prayer and supplication all things are possible, moreover, a lot of common sense and experience gives parents the right to lay foundations and set rules for their children to abide by.

It's tough being a youth in today's society; however, children can achieve and become the leaders that we need them to be tomorrow with good parenting.

By helping our children have positive self esteem, assisting them in setting goals, teaching them to analyze decisions and discussing drugs with them, we are equipping them with the tools they need to build the life they desire to have. Although mistakes will be made and lessons will be learned via trial and error, our since of duty as parents will be complete when we have done all that we can do.

www.ingramcontent.com/pod-product-compliance
Lightning Source LLC
Chambersburg PA
CBHW031254060726
47590CB00003B/906